It's a Wild life, buddy!

Daniela De Luca

BEN
THE BEAVER

Tommy NELSON

IN THE BEAVERS' LODGE, Mother Beaver was
making a fern-leaf pie. Her youngest kits were
helping, except for Ben. He was begging his father to take him
on the willow expedition. "Ben, you're just too young," Father
explained. Ben's older brothers and sisters chattered excitedly
as they got up ready to leave.

4

Young beavers, up to 12 months old are called "kits."

DO BEAVERS REALLY LIVE IN FAMILIES?

Yes, beavers stay in family groups made up of an adult pair and offspring from several previous years.

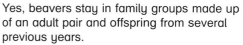

WHAT DO BEAVERS EAT?

They eat tender tree bark, tree roots, buds, ferns, grasses, and algae. Beavers are especially fond of poplars and willows.

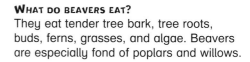

Bark

Tree roots

Fern leaf

Grass

Willows

Tender leaves

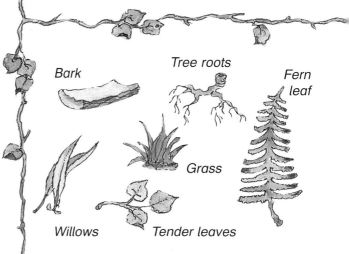

It was a beautiful fall afternoon, and Father Beaver hugged his wife before setting out. "Just raise the red flag if you need anything while I'm away," Father told her. Then he and the four kits left through the underwater door to their lodge. Ben tried to follow by sneaking around the side of the lodge, but he got caught up in the brush.

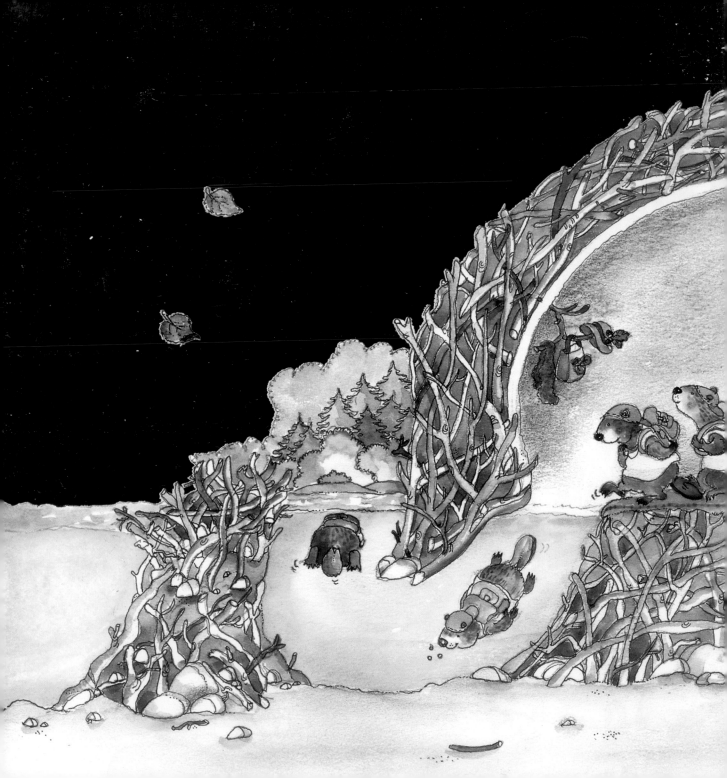

DO BEAVERS REALLY LIVE IN LODGES IN THE MIDDLE OF PONDS?
Yes, they even make the ponds themselves by building dams out of tree trunks and branches. Then they build their lodges in the middle, safe from predators.

7

WHEN BEN UNTANGLED himself from the brush he set off after his father and older brothers and sisters. The moon reflected across the big lake as Ben swam toward the faint sound of his family's voices. Soon, heavy rain began to fall.

DEEP IN THE WOODS, Father Beaver and the kits were surrounded by eyes peeping out of the leafy darkness. Suddenly, an owl hooted and the kits jumped! "Don't worry," Father told them, "We're surrounded by friends."

Do beavers really fell trees?
Yes, they gnaw around the base
of the trunk until the tree topples
over. They then use them to
build dams as well as for food.

14

Do beavers' teeth ever stop growing?
No, their teeth are constantly growing. So to keep them healthy, beavers have to keep gnawing all the time. This files them down into perfect tools for felling trees and eating.

AFTER SOME TIME BEN FOUND HIS FATHER and the kits. They were busy collecting willow wood for the lodge. It was raining even harder as Ben climbed a rock and spied the lodge in the distance. "Dad! The red flag!" Ben yelled. "Mom must need help!" Ben felt horrible. If he had stayed behind with Mother, he could be helping her now! Ben followed closely as his father raced back to the dam.

MOTHER BEAVER AND THE BABIES
were huddled together on top of
the lodge. They clutched their
favorite belongings, but many
things had already been
swept away. "Don't worry
little ones," Mother
said. "Help will
come soon."

16

SURE ENOUGH, Father Beaver and the kits were riding through the storm on a fallen log. They were on their way to rescue Mother Beaver and the babies.

DO BABY BEAVERS REALLY SWIM?
Yes, kits are able to swim just a few hours after they are born. But they are so small and fluffy at first that it is hard for them to go underwater. It takes a while before they can swim down the underwater passage and leave the lodge.

HOW LONG DO KITS STAY IN THE LODGE?
Mother beavers nurse their babies for about six weeks. All members of the family, especially the males, bring food back to the lodge for the kits to eat. Soon the babies begin leaving the lodge to swim in the lake, but they return every morning to sleep through the day. They leave the family lodge when they are about two years old to begin their own families.

BEFORE LONG the rain stopped and a beautiful rainbow appeared. Father and the kits pushed a big log into the dam, and the water stopped flooding into the pond. All the beavers cheered.

How big is a beaver's dam?
A beaver's dam can measure anywhere between 15 and 300 feet in length and can be up to 10 feet tall.

Do beavers really repair their dams?
Yes, beavers repair their dams year after year, and some are thought to be centuries old. Most dam-building is done at a time of high water in autumn and spring.

19

ALL THE BEAVERS' FRIENDS gathered sticks and
branches and carried them across the lake.
The beavers and their friends quickly rebuilt
the lodge. Beaver cousins
from far away all
came to help.

THE BABY BEAVERS were too small to help, but they found ways to enjoy themselves. Ben and his cousin Natalie played a game of Ping-Pong with a piece of the weeds as a ball. They used their tails as bats!

DO BEAVER FAMILIES WORK TOGETHER TO BUILD THEIR DAMS AND LODGES?
Yes. The adult females are the most active builders. Kits don't help with construction work until they are at least a year old.

WHERE DO BEAVERS LIVE AROUND THE WORLD?
As the map shows, beavers live in North America, Scandinavia, western and eastern Europe, central Asia, and northwest China. They were nearly wiped out by hunting in North America, but were reintroduced.

When the lodge was finished, the beavers decided to celebrate. But Ben was out on the doorstop gazing up at the night sky. Winter had come, and a light dusting of snow covered everything in sparkling white powder. "Ben, come inside where it's warm," Father called. Ben went inside to find a big party going on. He was happy his family was safe at home once again.

22

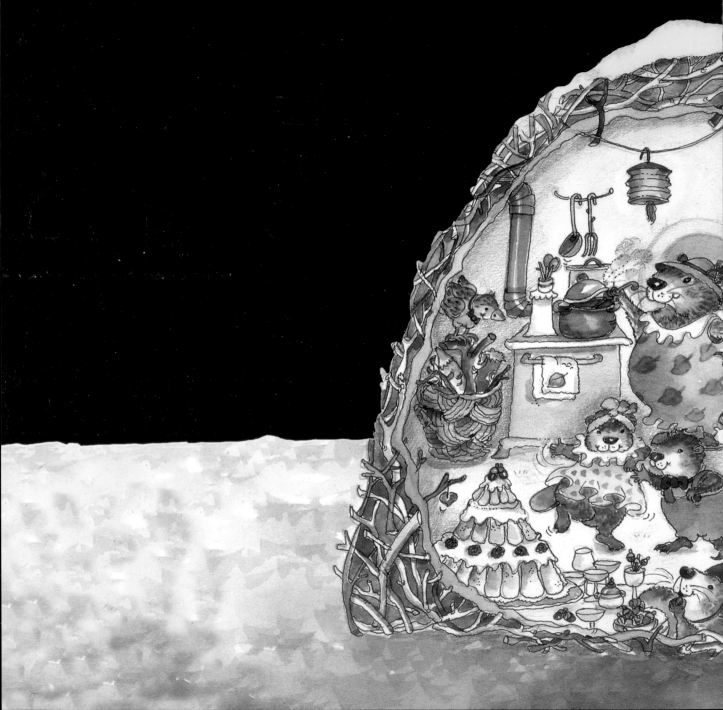

DID YOU KNOW?

LIKE ALL BEAVERS, Ben is a rodent. Rodents are a very successful group of animals and there are about 2,000 species of them living in the world today. Rodents live in a wide variety of habitats in every part of the world. Many, such as rats and mice, live alongside humans and are often considered as pests.

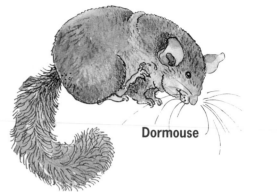
Dormouse

Squirrel

Chinchilla

Nutria

Urson

Mouse

Water Rat

Hamster

Gerbil

Marmot

Porcupine

25

THIS PICTURE SHOWS Ben posing with his friends. All these animals live in North America. Can you spot Ben? Do you recognize all his friends?

Canadian Goose

Grizzly Bear

Springhorn

Crane

Rocky Mountain Goat

Spoonbill

Prairie dog

Manatee

Turtle

Black Bear

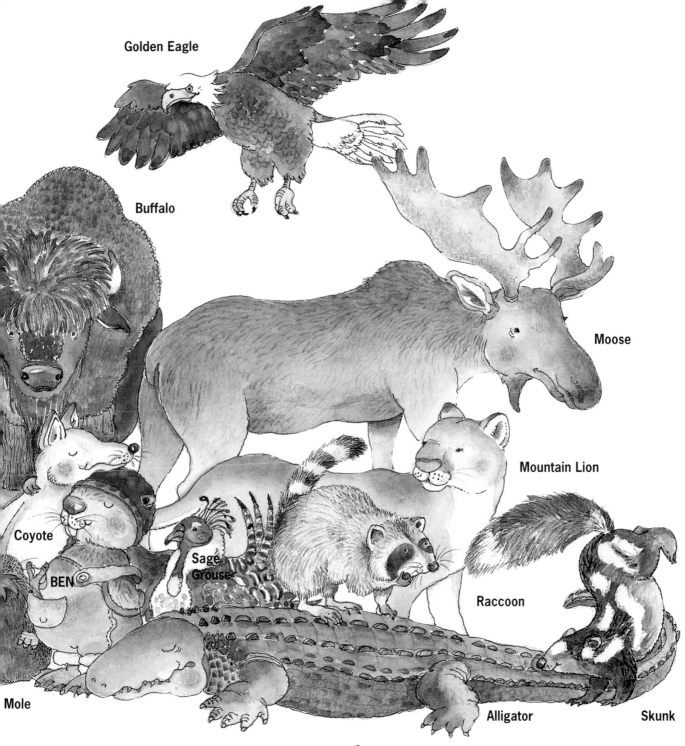

Golden Eagle

Buffalo

Moose

Mountain Lion

Coyote

BEN

Sage
Grouse

Raccoon

Mole

Alligator

Skunk

27

So God made the wild animals, the tame animals and all the small crawling animals. . . . God saw that this was good.
Genesis 1:25

Copyright © 2005 McRae Books Srl, Borgo S. Croce, 8 — Florence, Italy
info@mcraebooks.com

ISBN 1-4003-0604-3

Scripture quoted from the *International Children's Bible®, New Century Version®,* copyright © 1986, 1988, 1999 by Tommy Nelson®, a Division of Thomas Nelson, Inc., Nashville, Tennessee 37214.

This book was conceived, edited and designed by McRae Books Srl, Florence, Italy.

North American version published by Tommy Nelson®, a Division of Thomas Nelson, Inc.

Publishers: Anne McRae, Marco Nardi
Text: Vicky Egan
Illustrations: Daniela De Luca
Designers: Rebecca Milner, Sebastiano Ranchetti

05 06 07 08 09 — 5 4 3 2 1

Repro: Litocolor, Florence, Italy
Printed and bound in China